Apocalypse Soon

The Mostly Unedited Poems of

Ezra E. Lipschitz

Translated from the original Curmudgeon
by Nathan Brown

MEZCALITA
PRESS

MEZCALITA PRESS, LLC
Norman, Oklahoma

MEZCALITA PRESS, LLC
Norman, Oklahoma

Apocalypse Soon

Table of Contents

2 – *Among the Ruins*

3 – According to St. John the Divine

Introduction

It's curtains, folks.

Therefore, a toast to the inner curmudgeon as the priests and politicians light the fire beneath the stake he's been tied to.

Because, if a little honesty never hurt anybody… maybe a lot finally will.

~ Nathan Brown

June 2017

Acknowledgements

Ezra would like to thank Sierra Brown for keeping his real name, and the whereabouts of his cabin, a sworn secret.

Nathan would like to thank Ashley Brown for editing and, more importantly, putting up with the ridiculous amount of work and time he had to put into cutting, reshaping, and fixing Ezra's plethora of messes.

Also, and always, Christopher Everett for his awesome work in creating such fantastic book designs.

Mezcalita Press would like to thank John Roche for first publishing the poems "A Serious Laughter" and "What Remains" in the anthology *Survival* from the *Poets Speak Anthology Series*.

And again, Mezcalita Press wants to thank Donald Trump for pissing off Ezra enough that he finally agreed to allow these books to be published.

I looked through the Gideon Bible in my motel room for tales of great destruction.

~ Kurt Vonnegut
Slaughterhouse-Five

* * *

On prophets:

In ancient Israel they slew them with swords and staves and stones. Today we smother them more subtly, with vicious indifference, and bury them beneath the dust we allow to collect on the books that bear their names.

~ W. Randall Lolley
Journey with Me

Each person completely touches us
With what he is and as he is,
In the stale grandeur of annihilation.

~ Wallace Stevens
"Lebensweisheitspielerei"

Apocalypse Soon

Ezra E. Lipschitz

1 ...

A Serious Laughter

A Serious Laughter

When things are no longer funny,
I find humor to be the best weapon.

The world has lost its collective mind.
(Donald Trump was elected to be
president of the United States.)

But, this is not the first time.
Nor will this be the last—
we know how this works.

We know we're destroying
the planet each time we climb
into the car to go buy condoms.

And I'm talking about the condoms
as much as I am the engine fumes.
All that plastic packaging? Jesus.

But, we also know that babies
are egregiously more expensive
than the condoms we're off to get.

And I'm referring to the environment
as much as I am the empty pocketbook.
All of those disposable diapers? Christ.

We don't have a hell of a lot of time
to figure this stuff out, my friends.

That's why I mixed tequila, rum,

vodka, and gin here in the middle
of a hot, rain-soaked afternoon—
even though I prefer scotch—

a little something to help me
laugh, as I get more serious
about what I'm going to do
to try and help this world
(lost mind and caboodle)

that I've only recently
realized I love,
terribly.

Signing Off

When we lower that last flag
on the last day of the last days,

I think every set of bagpipes
in the world, with air left in it,
should play "Amazing Grace."

Something about that hard wind
in the brashest of instruments—
jackhammer of the music world,
the only thing that could've been
heard over a Scottish bar fight.

Something about the loudest
and harshest bag of reeds
and whiskied-up breath

playing the softest and
smoothest song we ever
ignored until it was too late.

Something about all the oxygen
it would suck from the atmosphere.

Something about all that hot air
to help accelerate the worst
parts of the very last
few minutes.

Head-scratchers

Alfred Bernhard Nobel, the man
who endowed the world's most
recognizable prize for peace
in 1901, invented dynamite.

His explosive little discovery
was rewarding enough for him
to set up the fund for the prizes
to go to those among us who have

conferred the greatest benefit on mankind.

Robert Lewis—then commander
of the Enola Gay, a retrofitted B-29
Bomber—wrote in his logbook,

My God... what have we done?

after dropping the atomic bomb
that liquidated Hiroshima in 1945
and carbonized over 150,000 souls,
burning their shadows on concrete
and steal, in a single white flash
hotter than a thousand suns.

President Harry Truman said,

*We have discovered the most terrible
weapon in the history of the world.*

He'd soon be wrong about that.

Then, J. Robert Oppenheimer,
creator of the terrible weapon,
puzzled us with these poetic
words upon its detonation,

*Now I am become death,
the destroyer of worlds.*

Paul Tibbets, the pilot
of the Enola Gay, said,

*Hell yeah,
I'd do it again.*

Mazel Tov!

When you live alone in woods
and have only three friends
who rarely check on you,

writing poems in the buff,
alone at your kitchen table,
with a cigar and big-ass glass
of lukewarm Purgatory Punch,

isn't something for anybody
to get all worked up about.

Who's going to know, until
the book is out next year?

I just left the "laureate"
at his house in Texas
to work on that sad
little book of prayers.

He seems all in a tizzy
about Climate Change
(he likes to capitalize it),

and I've come back home
to the mountains here to:

1) get away from him,

and,

2) give my own damn spin
   on the end of time.

Because, I believe
there are going to be
some breathtaking days

along with those scorchers
made of brimstone and fire
that burn in the last scene.

So, let us all join hands,
strip down to nothing,
and hoist our glasses
of this poison punch

to that great big hole
in today's ozone layer.

Concessions

For my first fifty years,
I had not considered that
I might have a front-row seat
to the biggest show the earth
has ever seen, except for
its traumatic birthday.

So, I'm trying to decide
which side of the Theater
of the Apocalypse to sit on.

Most General Admission folks
are aware that tickets are now
on sale, but they're not really
thinking this far ahead yet.

The liberal minimum-wagers,
college students, and otherwise
somewhat educated, are busy
still making their arguments
that he, whose name is not
worth mentioning, will be
the end of the world. But,
they know at least theoretically
our demise has long been slated.

The conservative minimum-wagers,
republican politicians, and likewise
generally uneducated, are busy
still making their arguments

that the big show is all hype
and won't even take place.

And yet they claim, religiously,
that Armageddon was promised
by a righteous and loving God.

As for me, I have been retired
for thirty years—from a job
I never had to begin with—

so, I've got time to decide
if I should be reasonable,

or just go ahead and order
that super-sized Dr. Pepper
and huge bucket of popcorn.

Beam Us Up

Dear Captain James T. Kirk,
of the Starship Enterprise,

never have we hoped
you might come true
more than we do now.

Even though your forced
and melodramatic delivery
was difficult to take at times.

Even though some of the costumes,
special effects, and those crazy dudes
with the massive throbbing egg-heads
were over the top.

              And yet, I must
admit that that very green alien
dancing slave girl was hotter
than we are all about to be.

(I believe the laureate even
wrote an ode to her once.)

O Captain! My Captain!
Where are you now…
in the hour of our ruin?

O Kirk… O Picard…
Skywalker, Han Solo!

We'll take anybody.

And, even though
I may have mixed up
my Star Treks and Wars,

we need a backup planet,
and we need it now.

And, we mean it
Obi-Wan Kenobi,

You're our only hope.

Dancing to the Stars

Therefore I tell you, do not worry
about your life, what you will eat
or what you will drink, or about
your body, what you will wear.

~ Matthew 6:25

I think Jesus would agree
that now is as good a time
as back then to be a Buddhist.

And so, for today, I refuse
to worry about my woes.

And I will grill this organic
all-beef hotdog, and pour yet
another glass of Purgatory Punch.

I vow to not exercise in any way,
and to do so with all my might.

And I shall shed all clothing,
down to my Brussels sprouts
and crocs with no-show socks.

And I shall blare the Bee Gees,
should I feel the need to do so,
here on this last short stretch
of the humid road to hell.

And, I think I shall also
"burn that mother down"
with The Trammps as well,
here in the final moments
of our big Disco Inferno.

For, it is my life after all
to refuse to worry about.

I think even Jesus would
snap his fingers and agree
that if we're going to burn
this whole mother down,

we should spin a kick-ass
groove and roller-skate out
with all our shotguns, pistols,
and big ol' mirror balls blazing.

Bucket List

There are ten things
I'll want to make sure
I get done, while I can.

One, try to use the pronoun
"I" three times in one sentence.
Ticked that box in the first stanza.

Two, reread the Book of Revelation.
Get a feel for how crazy it's gonna get.

Three, book a full tour and tasting
of every distillery in fair Scotland.

Four, track down, apologize to,
and make one last act of love
to Robin Bethel—the girl
I've known was the one
for over forty years now.

Five, take a last long cruise
that'll weigh anchor for a day
or two on the North Pole,
after all the ice is melted.

Six, draw a big "X" over
the front page of my 1040
Long Form with a big black
Sharpie, then fill in the blank

for Total Income: Fuck You.
And then mail it in to the IRS.

Seven, tell my daughter I'm sorry
for missing her first eighteen years,
but that, in the time since, she has
taught me that unconditional love
might exist outside the bounds
of sermons and silly platitudes.

Eight, and nine, are entirely
too personal for this book.

Ten, ask God to forgive me

   for not believing in him.

On Forgiveness... and about Time

I've been an angry man.
But I'm tired of it now—
as tired of it as anyone else
who knows me, I'd imagine.

It's 90° in February, so maybe
it's time to let some things go.

I need to forgive my parents
for the cultural and religious
bullshit, and the baggage that
was not necessarily their fault.
It was handed down through
the generations, genes, and
those backhands to the face
of angry European emigrants.

I need to forgive that first ex
for hiding a daughter from me.
And, for being one crazy-ass
(and I am toning this down)
bitch who refused therapy.

And it's past time to forgive
the second for her impatience
and dreadful short-suffering,
when I was trying... hard...
to recover my many losses.

But those are too obvious.
I should go a bit further...

I should even forgive Bob Dylan
for all the lyrics that sounded
stoned on his albums, but
looked twice as wasted
on the printed page…
    and The Beatles for
    paying teenaged girls
    to scream at their debut
    on the Ed Sullivan Show.

I shall also forgive the 80s
for Billy Idol, Kajagoogoo,
and that Flock of Seagulls…
    and even the 90s for being
    whatever the hell they were.

And maybe even Hollywood,
    for just about everything.

I mean, really, where could
the 21st Century have gone
except to the Apocalypse?

But, as for that bastard who
assaulted my only daughter?
The jury's still deliberating. Yes,

he may have to exit the stage early,
and by a trap door of my choosing.

Thinking Further Ahead

Sitting here in the back corner
of a smoldering coffee shop
in a desert college town—

half way between one place
and the next I need to get to
for some reason—and a cadre

of earnest finance and business
administration students squat
over S'mores Frappuccinos

and jabber about professors,
finals, and graduate programs
as if…

     as if any of it matters
    to their sweltering
    manifest destiny.

The Fourth Poet of the Apocalypse

...at the conference I'll never go to again

My friend, that poem was so long,
I had time to write three, before
you got to Section Four, of eight.

Man, that damn poem was so long,
I had time to order someone else's
book that I care about on Amazon.

Dude, that poem was so f-in' long,
I had time to go out and take a shit
before you made it to Section Six.

My God, that mother was so long,
I had the time to book a ride away
with Uber, before Section Seven.

And, my friend, I heard it from
one who didn't escape, that f-in'
Section Eight was even worse.

It's Time

Like the parent it took
up until her deathbed, or
his final day filled with IVs
and bedpans, to get to know,

I suggest we spend some time
with the earth, along the shores
of rivers and seas, walking with
the trees in her shrinking forests.

Learn to accept, and love, the sun
in late August—even if it kills us.
Take every slice of moon you get,
waxing, waning, or a perfect half.

Find a spring still clean enough
to draw from, cup your hands,
drink deep. Something in you
will stir, profound as an axe.

An axe that we both know
we should stop wielding,

for the trees that hope
we won't stop trying.

While It Burns

Like the pillar candle
burned down so far
and deep in its body
we can't see a flame,

but the soft yellow
glow still pulses
within its heart.

It is the light
we have left
to guide us...

dim as it may be.

All-Points Bulletin,

for the Arts and Sciences

Imagine the ocean with waves
made of orange and blue flames...

    or a huge thundercloud stalled out
    over the Great Plains. And so,
    the rain never stops falling.

Imagine the last eagle landing on a branch
in that last tree, after its last flight...

    or the last blue whale beaching,
    because the water's too hot.

Imagine earth looking like a round red
ember from the near side of the moon...

    or maybe just a ball of smoke, or fog.

Imagine your great granddaughter
being led to the gallows...

    and then... I beg you...
    spend some time thinking
    what your next move should be.

No Eden

As a kid, back in Colma, California,
sun and summer were my friends.

I loved and lived for it to break
through the smog and fog banks.

Now, even here in the mountains,
the sun and summer can beat you
like a drunk parent when you try
to run from the porch to the car.

And, when my Volvo runs out
of Freon, a road trip can feel
like cremation in slow motion.

Not long ago, I wandered along
the stony, cactus-laden backbone
of a hard and drought-stricken land
dead middle of some August day,
and I asked the no one there,

Whose garden was this?
And why did she abandon it?

Limber Up

The woman from Pasadena
has me doing yoga with her
some, now. She's concerned
my grumpiness may someday
metastasize, if I don't free it.

And because she's probably
as right as she is beautiful,
it made sense to at least try.

Besides, I'm tired of a body,
namely knees and shoulders,
telling me what I can't do.
Not anymore, anyway.

It turns out that cartilage
and bones have loud voices.
And they start to scream at you
when you pass a half century.

The thing is, they are none
too happy about yoga either.

I've never heard so much bitching
and moaning from my inner reaches.

But she says you've got to stick with
the practice for it to do any good.

And look, I may be grumpy...

but I am smart enough to realize
I need to limber up for the long
haul ahead in these latter days.

No telling how far we'll soon
have to walk to find fresh water.

What Remains

Today... I will celebrate
the snowmelt, laughing
here in the Navajo River

Today... I will sing along
with even the irritating cries
and caws of black crows
and the Mountain Jays

Today... I will drive
the backroads below
these snow-capped
Sangre de Cristos
that'll carry me down
to my daughter's eyes,
those shining quasars
in the darks of my skies

Today... I may even rhyme
a few of this poem's lines,
but then pull out before
it's literarily too late

Today... I will drink
the water while it's clean
enough not to kill me, and
the sacred scotch—as long
as Juan continues to pour it
at my end of Maria's little bar

Tonight… I will sit by
this popping piñon fire
and remember to mostly
listen to my girl's stories,
instead of offering all my
damn good advice to her

Tonight… I will praise
the Full Worm Moon
as it hovers up over
the same piñon fire

Tonight… I'll thank
a god I wish was there
for the high desert chill
and needle-whiff of pine

Tonight… I'll play a song,
a deep, river-bottom hymn,
to the American Southwest,
my plea to every earth-force
and power of benevolence
to help us save the glory
and wonder of this place

What Would It Take

The laureate has a long
John Denver playlist of songs
he believes could save the planet.

He is a bit naïve that way. And yet,
at the same time, I have my own list
of dirt roads, hikes, hidden highways,
here on the west side of the Rockies
that, I suppose, might do the same.

And though it embarrasses me
to admit, if we could get all
the people of the world
to combine the two?
We might just turn
the whole ship around.

We would cut the tops off
of our SUVs and convert them
into herb gardens and koi ponds.

We would dig up well-manicured
lawns, plant rows of pumpkins,
squash. And hemp, of course.

And religious types might quit
just quoting the damn scripture
and actually beat their swords
back into ploughshares.

My Favorite Scene

Sensing the changes
in the earth's atmosphere,

a tall spruce out by my fire pit
has decided to put on its finest.

I have seen a thousand angles
of sunlight mark its needles
throughout a single day.

And the moon hits it
with a thousand points
of silver light on clear nights.

And this is now the only movie
I truly care to watch anymore,

until the theater closes.

Here, by the Fire

Snow on the Southern Rockies
is my reprieve—a late spring
nip hanging in mountain air.

Whenever I venture out into
the world at large, and see
where progress's gotten us,

I'll hit some tipping point
and have to retreat back
to this haven in the pines.

Ten lanes blazing by a stream
of Taco Bells, outlet malls,
and Mitsubishi dealerships

depresses me, and I do not
think my childhood or general
disposition are solely to blame.

We fucked it up. But it's hard
to see it for what it is up near
80 mph in the far-left lane. So,

here, by this fire, my soul
stops holding its breath,
my corpuscles regroup.

Here, by the fire, I renew
my promise to no one at all
to go on living for a while.

And here, by the fire, even
a bastard like me wishes
for a someone like you

a chance to do the same
before it is past too late
for the both of us.

Light Your Arrows...
Load the Catapults...

"For it is important that
    awake people be awake,"
says the poet, William Stafford.

Though I might add "and that
    they stay awake, please."

This is not a time for liberals
to turn back to their arguments,
over goblets of wine, about Plato's
shadows flickering on the cave wall,

or for the moderates to roll back over
and return to their grog-infused naps.

It's all hands on deck, dear sailors,
everyone to post, my friends—
and my enemies as well.

The Trump is at the gate,
and his minions are quickly
surrounding the castle walls,

            and we are all
            about to die.

Atavism Maybe?

Did his parents accidently drop
the newborn sac of hot genes
and DNA on the way home
from the maternity ward?

Was he born with a tail?

How far back does he go?
Homo habilis?   Erectus?

Did his shoulders just lurch
forward during the debates,
his knuckles inching down
toward all that blue carpet?

Or was he performing some
odd mating ritual of a species
much further back than that?

Are there tests we could run?
Is surgery still a possibility?

Good God, dear doctors—
is there *anything* you can do?

The Next Frontier

The ego is the only thing
that worries itself over the earth
divesting its outer shell
of human life.

Homo finitus,
the last iteration of
a species that wanted
to believe it was in charge,

won't be remembered or mourned
by the next evolutionary step
of the Madagascar hissing
cockroach—but…

it will be missed
by the kissing bugs
that liked to suck on
our lips for the blood.

Otherwise I can imagine
what is left being happy
with some damn peace
and quiet for a change.

And the Sea Ghosts,
those fragile snailfish
down at 26,000+ feet
in the Mariana Trench,

won't even know
that we ever came along,
let alone that we ever went.

And though the planet's crust
will be hard-baked and burnt
all around the edges, I also
like to imagine the return
to some amount of beauty,

especially after the skyscrapers,
freeways, and big-box stores
have all disintegrated.

I. The Curmudgeon Blues

When the curmudgeon pauses
over his coffee on the porch
he built in the mountains...
it is not anger that he feels.

As if he sprinkles his cup
with a pinch of cynicism
and a dash of disdain.

It is a wide-angled pain
and sorrow he cradles for all
that goes unnoticed in the world.

And he's aware of his self-righteousness.
There is no illusion on the scene. He had
unnoticed it all himself—long enough
to cause this sad disappointment.

It is the weight of what a person
can't help another one see, when
the television is never turned off
and iTunes plays while we sleep,
that drives him to grumpy silence.

There was a good man in him,
if there isn't still. That's why
he wants to be left alone.

He's merely poking at
and rummaging around

in the detritus
of his life,

trying
to figure out
where he went.

II. The Hermit's Lament

When the hermit hesitates
over his chips between sips
of scotch, it is not in order
to fondle his lonely state.

As if this barren territory
was what he'd hoped for
all his long, pathetic life.

He has suffered losses,
within and without—
and so, he's just trying
to mitigate the damage.

There's a lot to sort out,
various piles to be made,
and he needs the space,
but especially the quiet,
for such a tedious task.

Therefore, keep in mind,
when you head out and up
on a sanctimonious mission
to save him from self-infliction,

you have missed the point,
even before you arrive.

As Stupid Does

With the look of a well-pickled
and preserved octogenarian,

the intelligence of a well-
purchased ivy education,

the emotional maturity
of a pouty third-grader,

the epic megalomania
of a spoiled Greek god,

the vocabulary of a honky
hip-hop-star-wannabe who
still lives in his old frat house,

and the communication style
of some kindergarten bully
out making his rounds
on the playground...

I'd say our future
is in good hands.

Her Left Hook

It is not for me, nor my own kicks,
that I write this book, Mister Trump.

I am over 60 and make little money.
I have no retirement and live alone
in a cabin as much in New Mexico
as it is in Colorado, since no one
drew a visible line between them.

I have my mind. I've got my health,
coffee, bread, beans, and a shotgun
for when I run out of one thing
or the other on that short list.

No, the book is for my daughter,
and all children and grandchildren,
who haven't had the chance yet
to become the savior of hell
that you quite appear to be.

You stand on your stump
and declare that this planet
is lying about the way she feels.

An opinion any moron may express.
But you—you have the power now
to help drive the knife in deeper
to her withering heart. And you,
with the flick of a brass pen, tilt
your head toward the camera

and scrawl with the smirk
of a spurned minotaur,
and twist her life away.

But beware, ye fiend...

if she rallies at the end?

She will swallow you up
with her molten tongue
in a red tunnel of fire,

then suck you back
down where you
came from.

I'll Take It

I'm struggling with whether it would be
irresponsible, verging on cruel, to bring
a child into this world, as it is now...

My daughter springs this on me.

So I say, For what reasons, Hon?

All of them, she says. Because she
is a first-rate smartass. About which
there is nothing I can say, of course.

So I ask first, Are there any positives?

Love, she answers, without a pause.

I quiver a bit and say, Well... yeah...
I can't fight you on that one, Sweetie.

She says thank you without using words.

But Dad, the seas are rising, the rivers
are about to boil. And the air is going
to get harder to breathe, anon, et al.

Now, Honey, those aren't certainties.

Well, you've done the research, she says.
So tell me, how much doubt do you have?

I don't answer, pleading the pouring
of my second cup of coffee instead.

Mhm. That's what I thought.

After an appropriate wait, I ask,
Would there be a father involved?
And if so, would I know who he is?

I get an eye-roll and a head-shake sigh.
Dad… you know that doesn't matter.
Not anymore. There're ways around.

Well, it used to matter, I regretted,
the instant it flew out of my mouth.

My daughter's had a difficult time
with men—because she is wickedly
funny, quick-thinking, excruciatingly
intelligent, and she carries herself
with all the grace and beauty
of a citizen of Olympus.

So… intimidating,
one could say.

A thing I am pleased
as all Hawaiian Punch about.

So I say, This is one of those times,
Honey, when a father wishes

like crazy to be fatherly,
and therefore, offer some sort
of fatherly-ish advice that would
make him the best father in the land.

But, you are too smart not to know
that there is no answer to this one,
this rather uniquely 21st-Century
conundrum for the coming age.

She walks over to bury her face
in my left shoulder, and it feels
like a minor victory, for once.

Drink with Me

Life'll be about water. Soon.

That stuff we leave running?
On the lawn? While we head
to the store to buy more of it
that is clean enough to drink?
The store that's running low?
The grass that died anyway?

Hold onto your hoses, folks.
All the aquifers are caving in
while the acid oceans rise—
and we'll soon start wishing
we could get a few thousand
of those gallons back, maybe
before the next Ides of March.

The hippies have known this
since their revolution began:
Only wash your underwear
when you go to visit mom.

The silvery fish are making
flashy billboards by floating
on their sides along the shore.

And ask a dead camel's hump
what it means to run dry—
then, raise your last glass
as if it were champagne.

Who's Who

My fellow older people—
     and by older I mean
     whatever you want
     to believe—

we need to stop bitching
about younger people—
     and by younger I mean
     their knees don't hurt yet
     and they still have dreams.

Stop the griping about
their attention spans
and lack of work ethic,

and realize that if you think
they don't have anything worthy
to say or contribute to a dying world,
it's because you don't believe they could.

Maybe think instead about how soft
and gelatinous your ass is getting
while you sit in that easy chair
and bitch at Fox News, or
MSNBC, about those damn
planet-kissing-vegetarian liberals,
or those money-grubbing, methane-
spewing conservatives, and realize that
it may be you who has nothing worthy
to say or contribute to a dying world.

I have a sense that younger people
might want to live their lives
during something besides
the Apocalypse.

And, I am certain
that older people have
a hell of a lot less to lose.

So, think about maybe
getting off that soft ass
and putting it on board
the fix-this-thing train
the younger people
need you on.

Or...   if not...

maybe quit sucking up
all their valuable oxygen.

Life Among the Skunks

As much as I love the woman
from Pasadena—and, I do...
she's one of the truer things
I have ever felt, instead of
thinking it to death—

I will never shake off
my deep-bred desire
to go to bed... and
then, wake up alone.

Some may see it as sad.
But, this earth has been
enough for me, and will be.

For the humans I've known,
an ancient pine tree is as solid
a companion as any—a skunk
is even better than most, since
his bullshit is so predictable.

And, yes, I feel a twinge
of something every time
she pulls out to head back
to that part of California
I will never understand.

But, she had no more
intention of staying here
than the flock of grey geese
down by the muddy pond does.

They'll be back, come next fall,
but only and ever on their terms.

So, among the better things a man
can hope for anymore, is to drink
his scotch and fart in peace...

and then, die here
in the steadfast arms
of these giant ponderosas.

A Conversation

This is John, he said
into his cell phone.

John, hey man, this is Jim,
the phone's speaker said.

Hey there, John and Jim, I said,
loud enough for both of them,
and the others in the coffee shop.

John looked my way, then said,
Hey Jim, how are things going there?

And before Jim got a word out,
I said, *Not good, John… not good.*

John looked over my way again,
and said to me, *What're you doin'?*

John, and Jim, if you can hear me,
I said, *I am out raising awareness
about how obnoxious little fuckers
like you two are, who carry on phone
conversations at the public's expense.*

His phone beeped a few times.

I believe Jim has left us, John, I said.

A girl in the corner laughed out loud.

A man to my left applauded, softly.

John gave me a good hard glare,
but then got up and left anyway.

A woman across the room
looked over and mouthed,
without sound, *Thank you.*

2 ...

Among the Ruins

Comeuppance

The mistake
was in believing
the earth was ours,

that it somehow owed
Homo sapiens perpetuity.

And just because we gave
all the animals of the world
names that they didn't need,

does not insinuate that they
owe us a damn thing either.

The Book of Genesis instilled
in humans a rather deadly
sense of superiority…

and we will certainly pay,
down to the very last penny
in the bottom of our pocket,
for that error in judgment.

The Ruin

There is a corrugated cross
the size of a small skyscraper
among the windmills, cactus,
and tumbleweeds just east
of the 72-ounce steak
in Amarillo, Texas.

A zealous attempt
to create a constant
reminder that Jesus
was dead serious
about the whole
dying thing.

And if the stuff
it's made of doesn't
melt at 150°, it'll remain
long past the last man
standing on earth—

a righteous and rugged
middle finger pointing up
to a scorched and empty sky.

In Ruins

There is a cattle yard
the size of a small suburb
among the weeds and yucca
just west of that same steak
over in Amarillo, Texas.

The smell is a constant
reminder, especially when
the wind is out of the south,

of what a trillion Big Macs
with a side of greasy fries
have done to our upper
and lower intestines.

My Ruin

There is a billboard on I-40,
355 miles west of Arizona,
with a huge 800 number

      FOR TRUTH

I'm feeling the urge.

And I'm pretty sure
I won't get Trump
on the other end.

Though I'd give
my right testicle
for such a chance.

But whoever answers,
the truth on my end
will be that I won't
give a shit what
they have to say.

I'll just talk, until
they finally hang up.

Avoiding Ruin

There is a dusty two-lane blacktop
on the better side of the Rockies
they call the Cosmic Highway.

It stretches straight up north
out of Alamosa, Colorado.

And in the statutory town
of Hooper, you can stop in
for a curio and walk along
the UFO Watchtower®,

where you can scan 360°
of the San Luis Valley—
a forsaken view of mostly
jackrabbits and tumbleweeds.

Still, when the goin' gets too hot
here on the surface of our blue ball,

I'm gonna make a B-line back to this
outpost and hitchhike my way
to some other galaxy.

It Could Happen

Could Trump awaken somehow
enough of us from the great
sleep of affluent oblivion

to jumpstart our desire
to block all cocks like his
from raping what little's left
of our hope and our Mother?

Could he, and his horny legions,
frighten enough good fathers that
they finally decide their daughters
are at least as important as their
Second Amendment rights?

Could his ego erection
swell to the point that
it turns purple and pops?

Could the wings of his hair
get stiff enough that the hot
and mighty wind of Congress
blows him so far off the shore
that he could not swim back?

And could he someday tweet
something so fucking stupid,
even the white supremacists
wash and fold their sheets?

Or, could God himself

get fed up enough
that he rains down
holy fire from heaven,

proving wrong everything
I have ever disbelieved?

Everything Mattered

We just couldn't figure out
that everything mattered.

Every little match we lit.
Every toilet we flushed.
Every hormone-infested
cow with bad gas in every
shit-strewn livestock yard.

Every Ziploc® baggie and
cellophane wrapper we put
inside a plastic grocery sack
to later shove inside the larger
heavy-duty trash bag we tossed,
only half-full, into the poly-cart,
for them to haul to the landfill.

Every leaf blower, gas mower.
Every electric edger, hedge
trimmer, and chainsaw.

Yes… for every degree
we cranked down the air
to make our restaurants
and movie theaters feel
a bit more like Norway…

for every 7,500-square-foot
McMansion we built for two
older people to live in, who

were never going to go up
those damn stairs anyway…

and for every tank, Hummer,
and wide-axle pickup we raised
to put on tractor tires, because
of shriveled identities and dicks,

there would be a price to pay.

And if this doesn't feel like
poetry to you, don't think
that it does to me either—

I just had something to say.

And it felt like it mattered.

Raven to Baker Team

Big situations
call for the big guns.

So, I'm pulling the trigger:

RAMBO FOR PRESIDENT

Eliminate the salaries of all
senators and representatives,
and send them home to play
with the tiny toy train villages
they build in their basements.

Cut health insurance benefits
for all government officials.

Assign federal judges only
cases that actually matter—
reducing the workload 93%.

Transfer the balance of funds
to the Seals and Green Berets,
and let John J. Rambo proceed
to sneak out into the bushes
and the jungles of the world
and, one by one, invisibly,

remove all those despotic
mongers running amok
with power and greed.

And though I refuse
to name any names,
we could start with:

Milo Yiannopoulos,
Kim Crazy-ass Jong-un,
and Vladimir What's's-face.

Want Ad

One used-up planet
   with a thousand
   burning Romes

seeks any available
all-powerful god
with enough time
and long-suffering

to save its ass from
the never-ending
atrocities of one
highly confused
and distracted
species.

In or Out

So, we know there is only
so much shit we can shove
down the earth's esophagus
before she throws it up, or
poops it out the other end.

It is the unavoidable way
digestive systems work.

And anyone who doesn't
understand this is wasting
much-needed living space
by continuing to sit around.

And yet… even in dying,
they would still just be
more shit to shovel
into her throat.

Down to the Core

I burn books…

books I cannot believe
I gave five minutes, let alone
the hour I usually do, because
I wanted to give them a chance.

A disorder the laureate and I share.
And we admit the reason is to free up
shelf space—it's just too valuable here
at the dawn of the great downsizing.

If the act offends you, think of it
as a ceremonial way to cleanse
the world of mediocrity—
a critical service project.

If not, I will likely continue
to toss 'em on the fire anyway.

It turns out that academic poetry
burns brighter and faster—probably
because of the hubristic ejaculate
smeared all over the pages.

Volumes III, IV, and V
of Proust's roman-fleuve,
    In Search of Lost Time,
didn't ever catch flame.

They just turned to coal.

Ginsberg took freakin' forever,
and is still smokin' down in the pit.

Dean Young and John Ashbery
dimmed the light for a time,
like damp cedar wood.

So, I've got a little extra
space now, if you happen
to have any recommendations.

Said and Done

I see a dark future world
of burning books—some era
when there's no one left to read
the few we ever understood.

I see the charred remains
of libraries and bookstores.

A few copies of ol' Trump's
The Art of the Deal, the only
hardbacks to beat the heat
of the apocalyptic flames.

Shit turns to stone in time.

I see the Jefferson Building
on First Street in D.C.—
the Library of Congress—

a torched and crumbling
monument to the truth
we'd come so close to
figuring out before
it was too late.

Fatherland

I love my country
the way a grown son
might love a famous parent
who is a more notorious drunk.

I attend some of the big parties
with him, try to be something
good that came from him.

I shake hands... smile...
tell those other countries
he's got his better qualities.

But they see me drinking too.
Just a little less of the stuff—
so I can help him to the car.

Others did once love him.
Some of them still might.

It's been a good ride,
and I can't imagine
what I will do...

when he's gone.

A Closing Scene

I recall a certain scene
from James Cameron's
questionable rendition
of *Titanic* back in 1997—

a sad-ending date I allowed
a once-lover to coax me into.

Still, it might have been worth
that one scene, the one where
the older elite, the obscenely
wealthy in their tuxes and
waxed shoes, diamonds
and shimmering dresses,

are sitting calmly at tables
in the ornate dining room,
that part of the ship no one
else is allowed into, because
the insanely rich do not die
in such situations as piddly
as catastrophic shipwrecks.

They would be fine, while
all of the others drowned
around them. Fine because
obscene amounts of money
always float in times like this.

Yes. The looks on their faces
when the Atlantic smashed
the windows and the frigid
salt water came rushing in
and swirled in huge eddies
around their pedicured toes.

That's it. The look I imagine
on the rhinoplastic touch-ups
of the supremely affluent when
they realize there is no more
artesian well water to drink,
the sky is turning to fire,
and the air, to sulfur.

The Circa Espresso Bar

The Circa coffee shop at the end
of the Historic Route 66 Motel
out in Tucumcari, New Mexico,

serves "The Atomic Espresso,"
an "Ice Cold Ballistic Blast,"
on the days they are open.

The décor exhibits overt
nostalgia for the early years
of the Cold War with Russia.

Postcards feature sultry women
dressed like Jackie O and antique
photographs of mushroom clouds.

Two marble pillars by the bathroom
display authentic Geiger Counters
that read radiation levels in the 50s.

And, the west wall is covered with
Civil Defense Manuals from the 60s
and big posters explaining how to

build bomb shelters, and how to
protect yourself in the coming
Radioactive Fallout—and even

one on measuring preparedness,
from First Aid to knowing your
radio stations and warning signals.

All reminiscent of the good ol' days
when children crawled under desks
in abject terror, little girls weeping

uncontrollably, little boys crying
while staring at the white panties
of the little girls in front of them.

And if the world weren't burning
down all around us now, but for
other reasons, this little joint,

with its creepy theme and
maudlin interior design,
would almost be cute.

How You Look at It

I rode the Purple Heart Trail
most of the day, along with
a section of The Devil's Rope
through the heart of Santa Rosa,

       thorn-grass desert,
       yucca-chollo plains,

      drought-dry fence posts
      with corroded barbwire,

     a rattlesnake wriggling
     in the Red-tail's talons,

    this pebble-dust infinity
    some might want to claim
    isn't worth saving anyway.

But I say, down to the mufflers
and beer bottles in the ditches,

any god would be crazy
to let all this go.

Get on It

Wildflowers
and deciduous trees
are blooming and budding
a month early this winter.

A wildly radiant sight
to witness, no doubt.

And I will not dwell
on what an ominous
and grave omen it is.

But, if you're hoping
to ever ski again…

    I'd make plans
    sooner, rather
    than later.

The End Begins…

…with ants taking over our kitchens
    and wasps invading our attics

…when people believe the Real
    Housewives of Bravo Network
    are, somehow, real housewives

…where the garbage trucks unload

…when our president can't spell
    a fucking three-letter word

…where polar bears no longer
    have an ice block to stand on

…when Aztlán, the legendary
    homeland of the Aztecs,
    is made a brand name
    for spaghetti squash

…when great songwriters
    appear in commercials
    for luxurious sedans

…with the whimper
    of complacency

…as a dictator smirks
    directly into the camera

…possibly, right where the Bible

says that it would

...with a complete lack
   of any solid evidence

...just inside the boundary
   of the yellow caution tape

...when terror cells of God's
   finest have absolutely
   nothing to lose

...with as little as
   one more degree
   on Mercury's gauge

What Will No Longer Matter

...the number of calories from fat

...the blurbs on the back cover

...composting, or recycling

...those damn republicans

...nor the damn democrats

...whether this is the second
   or the third glass of scotch

...the other guy who wants her

...the ingredients on the label

...winning the Pulitzer Prize

...the Tenth Commandment

...the volume on the car stereo

...that damned Oxford comma

...a critic's opinion of this book

...nor yours, for that matter

Ash and Ore

I'll light a bonfire
for the final meltdown.

All two of my friends and I
will sing to the melodies
of our burning guitars
and their steel strings
slowly turning back
into liquid pig iron.

And when the volcano
beneath Yellowstone blows,
we'll strip down to nothing
and dance in the hot rain
of ash and glowing lava.

We'll have no whimpering
or regrets in our small circle.

We brought this on ourselves.
So, let's celebrate our mistakes.

The unnecessary future will be
for the aliens and dung beetles
to discover, shake their heads,
and then rummage through.

Each One Counts

A cool morning here,
after the Ides of March.

And though our Caesar
is still alive and golfing
down at Mar-a-Lago…

there are pillowy clouds
and the tickle of a breeze
easing along the back side
of my favorite mountains.

A purple finch is cracking
open a pine cone to dig
for those musty seeds,

and the Navajo River
still has water rolling
over big black stones.

So… let us call today
a victory in the hot war
for what's left of the world.

A Place to Start

I heard an expert call it
the "Anthropocene"—
something about the first
epoch in geochronology
that's our own damn fault.

Like the Jurassic period,
or, say, the Paleozoic era,
with their mass extinctions.

Except this one, it appears,
will have to do with ours.

And, he got the term
from some scientist
who came before him,
because original thought
is rather hard to come by.

But I think naming it matters,
gives us some place to start—
to start considering things like
what the hell to do about it—

or how to pack our suitcases
for that very, very long cruise
through space to the next place.

The Coming Currency

Keep in mind, as you consider
your next move in mutual funds,
markets, stocks, and all their bonds,

money will no longer be the primary
means of exchange when there is
no water to drink in California.

English Ivy will be growing up
the inside walls of Wall Street,
and the cherry trees of D.C.
will all be picked bone-clean.

The president will be hiding
in an extravagantly-stocked
bunker he failed to inform
his supermodel wife about,

and the kids'll just have to
hitchhike over to Russia—
    where there will not be
    any water left either—
    except in remote parts
    of far Eastern Siberia.

The terms *droughtresistant*
and *flashflood* will become
one long word each,
without hyphens,

and the only thing
that will matter now,
will be your zip code.

Though mail delivery
will most certainly be
out of the question.

Burning Down the Castle

I imagine that very last day
looking something like
the very last hour
of a Medieval Fair
that's closing early
on account of rain.

The knight-in-clanging-
armor who has one last bar
of signal and decides to use it
to call mom back in Pittsburg.

The princess with black muck
on the hem of her pink dress
who is yelling at her father,
the king, to fix all this.

The beggar gnawing
on a turkey's fat thigh,
by gripping the hip bone,
because someone dropped it
when they heard the bad news.

And the joker passed out drunk,
because the joker's always been
smarter than everyone else.

You Don't Say

I whistled passed a graveyard
along Route 66 in Arizona.

Which one, and what town,
aren't important. And the road
isn't important either. I just like
Route 66 and wanted to namedrop.

But I thought about those dead-quiet
citizens and what they would not say
to me now… if given the chance.

I doubt they would tell me
Put it all in hedge funds… or

*Do not marry that wonderful
woman who visits from Pasadena.
You'll have a hundred better options.*

And, I don't think they'd say,
*Let it go. It's too late to be of help
or service to your daughter… or*

*Don't bother writing these books.
Because, it's too late for poetry too.*

One Way to Do It

Good Friday, early morning,
and the Penitentes are making
their slow, hot way to Chimayó.

On foot. They hail from all four
directions—some as far away
as a hundred miles. On foot.

They are slowing, spiritually,
metaphysically, the planet's
rotation on its crooked axis.

Some do the last bit down
on their knees. A few drag
rugged wooden crosses—

carry photos of loved ones
in trouble... or worse...
but all at this turtle's pace,

showing us along the way
what could save the world,
if we'd slow down with them.

News from the Western Slope

Reporting from The Bean
at 7,703 feet on Main Street
here in Gunnison, Colorado.

Coffee's hot, toes are cold,
and the kids are looking at
ski conditions on laptops.

A well-dressed family by
the front window speaks
about Jesus rising yet again
on yet another Easter Sunday.

The girl behind me is studying
about leading and lagging strands
in our DNA, and the limitations
that are imposed by synthesis.

Everybody seems to know
every-other-body else here,
and not one seems worried
the world is about to end.

*   *   *

Live, at the Coffee Trader
on Main Street in Montrose,
in a back room of the upstairs
in the old house where they
trade coffee for cold cash,

there's a real grumpy old dude
(and I don't mean me this time)
back at a table in the far corner

wearing his English tweed cap
pulled down over big fuchsia-
colored horn-rimmed glasses
and long salt-n-pepper hair
falling around a thick goatee

who is communicating with
the screen of an ancient and
battered Gateway computer
through a series of grunts
and deep, hoarse grumbles.

So, by all appearances…
he knows what's coming.

      *   *   *

Folks at the Happy Belly Deli
here in downtown Norwood
would rather you not bring up
global warming or climate change
or whatever the hell you wanna call it.

There's snow on Groundhog Mountain
and the wind's still pretty damn chilly
here in the later days of April.

So, they have other concerns,
like starting to collect firewood
for next winter, and the fact that
the mountain lions are beginning
to get more and more personal.
A little too… if you ask some.

Therefore, best eat your chili
in peace, and while it's hot—
otherwise keep your concerns
about the planet to yourself.

      *   *   *

It is a rare day in Telluride
when the streets aren't packed
with snow or tourists either one.

Makes the place almost bearable.
And, the sunshine on the sidewalk
out in front of The Coffee Cowboy
almost makes a hermit consider
hanging around town a while.

But Page 1 of the Daily Planet
tells me the laureate is in the area.
So, I'll have to slip the surly bonds
before he finds out I'm available
and invites me to some reading.

Page 13 claims "Julian Lennon

honors the environment in kids' book."

And, glancing back over on Page 12,
I notice a "newly discovered species
of shrimp..." has been named
for Pink Floyd—Holy crap.

The back page, which they call
The Second Front Page (clever)
carries this riveting headline:
"Smoke 'em if you got 'em."

You know, Telluride was once
such a cozy dive back before
the West Coast invaded
the Western Slope...
I loved this village.

But, as happens with
insanely gorgeous vales,
the wealthy have landed,
renovations are under way,
and... as far as I can tell...

more money than Solomon
ever had to sort and squander,
has postponed the Apocalypse.
At least for this happy hideout.

Out There

There's this small coffee shop
on Main in Roswell, New Mexico
that claims the aliens came here,
yes, that they chose this hot-ass
desert town for the sole reason
of the beans and hand-brews
they grind and pour in the back.

And there is a crazy old redhead,
smackin' the shit out of a beat-up
classical guitar over by the wall,
goin' on about how she just
got out of jail and has lost
400 pounds with a gastric
bypass she'd done right
before she went in—
and she's feelin' great
and ain't gonna take
no shit off o' no-
body no-more,
dammit.

And, if she
is any indication
of the clientele 'round here,

I guess they're right…
                              about the aliens.

Too Soon

~ for J. L.

Endings come in many forms—
and sometimes unimaginable
versions and variations—

to the good, the worse,
and the wealthy alike,
but certainly the poor.

I spend these months
bitching about fracking,
CEOs, and the plummeting
American intelligence quotient,
all for the sake of this book
on the end of the world,

then find out a friend
is having to have fluids
pumped out of his lungs
before the cancer deals
its final cell alteration.

And now I'm thinking,
What kind of putz am I…
sitting here writing this crap?

For him the Apocalypse is now.
So, he's not too worried about
one more plastic grocery bag
floating in the Pacific Ocean.

He needs morphine.
He needs sleep.

And, he needs
a lot more than
the Angel of Death
is going to let him have.

Hell, what he wouldn't give
for just a few more smog-filled
weeks of relatively mild pain.

A Good Ol' Night

Major James stopped by
on the way to his tiny cabin
where he hides out in Chama.

We talked around the fire pit
about fly fishing, and a rise
in black bear encounters.

On round two of scotch,
he had words for Trump
that surprised even me.

On a third, that night
in Lebanon came up,
back in late 1982.

And while I poured
a sip more in each glass,
we agreed the good ol' days
were never any such damn thing.

Hermitess

The dark lady from Durango
mystifies and comforts me
with her exquisite need
for absolute isolation.

Or what I think I meant
was, her absolute need
for exquisite isolation.

She makes me look like
a right man-about-town,

which makes her deceptively
easy to rarely ever go and visit.

She's like reading a one-page
Wallace Stevens poem—

you think you're almost,
maybe, going to get it
this time...
                then come
            those last few lines.

Out of the Way

The girl from West Virginia
wants to stop in on her way
through, to which I said,
No one passes through
this little mountain vale.
One only goes very much
out of one's way to get here.

Besides that, my shotgun and I
go out of our way to make sure
one is actually welcome first,
on the rare occasion that
any one stops in on us.

I can see her eyes rolling
on the other end of the line.

She says, Seriously.

I say, Me too.

She says, I want to tell you
that I am sorry.

I say, For how many things.

She says, Dammit, Ezra.

I say, Yes. All to hell.
Because, you were not

good for me. But, worse,
you hurt my sweet Jenny
when you ducked and ran.

She says, I know. I'm sorry.
I hated it then. I hate it now.

I say, As did, and does, Jenny.

She says, Look, some things
are different now—things
are changing, profoundly.

I say, No, things're ending.
In fact, all things are ending.

And, 'profoundly' will not
be near the word for it.

She says, I'll be there,
in a couple of weeks.

Passing Through

8:00 am on a Saturday
at a stale coffee shop,
in a town that I only
ever pass through,
and I am reminded,

the loneliness of cities
and towns is meaner
and more desolate
than the loneliness
of the mountains.

Squirrels and blue jays
are such better company
than a disenchanted barista.

A wet granite boulder has more
personality than some hipster
who was up all night long
because he lost at love
and couldn't sleep,
and now he's sitting
in a corner scribbling
mopey songs and poems
in a beat-up spiral notebook.

And I don't feel sorry
for either one of them.

We're all just surviving
in the fallout of concrete
sidewalks and rubber soles
and our parquet floors—

or any other damn thing
that divorces our feet
from the grass
and the dirt.

What the Santa Ana Winds Blew In

Another Californian
with nothing else to do
with the millions left her
in the divorce settlement,

has bought the shabby lot
across from my daughter's
and is leveling the old adobe
that had been there for over
a hundred years, give or take.

And Hell, as I've pictured it,
will crawl with backhoes,
bobcats, and bulldozers,
busy making room for all
the Devil's new recruits.

Soon there will be more
than even he'd hoped for.

In the meantime—the lady
from California will contract
a sleek new, glass-crazed,
modern piece-of-crap
that will look a lot like
a day trader standing out
in a West Texas cattle yard.

Praise be to good coastal ideas.

And then,
she will move in.

She'll stop dyeing her hair
and start wearing black silk
broom skirts, turquoise boots,
and handwoven vests covered
in hammered silver conchos.

And, her ex's monthly check
will buy her all the overpriced
jalapeño-infused margaritas
she could ever put away,

till the earth runs out
of turquoise, limes,
and salt.

3 ...

According to
St. John the Divine

Shortly

> The Revelation of Jesus Christ, which God gave
> unto him, to shew unto his servants things
> which must shortly come to pass;

> ~ Revelation 1:1

Shortly. That word reminds me:
no harbinger of doom ever says,
But worry not, my friends, these things
shall come to pass so far into the future,
your generation need not worry about it.

That would be bad for business,
because we'd all just turn back
to our TVs and iPhone screens.

Maybe this is why I'm suspicious
of scientists writing grant proposals
to help further their research on how
and when we deserve to die for our sins
against the earth. I don't think they're lying,

unlike politicians and golfers, but people
won't write checks or vote for you,
if you don't scare them enough.

But, I'm going to take more
time to think this through,

and I'll get back to you,
shortly.

A Dirty Revelation

I walked the manic streets
of New York City not long ago,
for reasons I don't even understand.

I was a bit overwhelmed with what
I thought I knew about the place,
because of strange, movie-related
moments of partial recognition.

And all the while, I was treated
with a magnificent indifference.

It's shocking how an encounter
as intimate as a stranger shoving
a flyer for a nudie club in your hand
can feel, only minutes later, so much
like nothing had actually happened.

Except for advertising, the scene
seemed like a mass experiment
in total non-communication.

And no one threw change
to the shoeless prophets
on the filthy sidewalks.

Bibles sat on a few shelves,
and in every hotel drawer,
gathering mold and dust.

And I could swear I saw
a message from some
unemployed angel
scrawled in black
on the smog.

But not a soul
was paying
attention.

My P's and Q's

Grace be unto you, and peace,

~ Revelation 1:4

…though, you, and all of us,
are still going to fry and burn
in the swelling sun's iron skillet.

But, that doesn't mean it wasn't
a nice thing for John the Divine
to say there in the opening lines
of the Book of the Apocalypse.

Though he likely didn't write it.
And, he was likely stoned when
he didn't. YouknowwhatImean?

That said, I too would like to say:

Grace be unto you, and peace,

in these fine, sunshiny days
before God's blowout
retirement party.

"In the Spirit"

I was in the Spirit on the Lord's day,

~ Revelation 1:10

So, Saint John is "in the Spirit,"
and turns around to the sound
of a great voice, when he sees
the seven golden candlesticks.

And, in their midst, he also
beholds some guy who is

"girt about the paps
with a golden girdle,"

hair white as wool, and
eyes that look like flames.

He has stars shooting out of
his right hand and a two-edged
sword coming out of his mouth,
while his whole countenance
shines forth like the sun.

And ye Christians,
priests and nuns
of my youth,
still think pot
should be illegal?

In the Wake

Just so there are no gray areas,
it was the priests and the nuns
I mentioned earlier, along with
the one or two bishops, and most
every other member of Holy Angels,

that served as the collective reasons
I lost interest, if not faith, in God.

And I know Gandhi already said
something along these same lines.
And I'm sure he was not the first.

And, know that I did not set out
to lose interest or faith. I wanted
to work things out—keep in mind,
my mother's faith and interest in God
was what kept her from being altogether
a terrible and wholly unbearable person.

God rest her soul—just in case
I am wrong about all of this.

And God rest mine—if good
intentions count for anything.

But, even to a kid's eyes, the nuns
and bishops looked like a band of
disenchanted, disappointed souls
that came together to bond
by the common flame
of commiseration.

As with Laodicea

So then because thou art lukewarm,
and neither cold nor hot, I will
spue thee out of my mouth.

~ Revelation 3:16

The folks at the church in Laodicea
did not corner the market on this,
a state of maddening mediocrity.

Stale dark roast continues to be
a problem in the greasy cafés
and diners of this country.

As does the poetry here,
likely because the poets
are drinking too much
of that stale coffee.

And, the prophets
are high, or drunk
on Johnnie Walker.

So... frankly...

I am amazed
we've lasted
this long.

Checklist

behold, a door was opened in heaven:

~ Revelation 4:1

We'll be looking for this door
when all the doors of earth
begin to close in our faces.

Ten billion people won't just
lie down and die in the streets.

And the moment we walk through
that door in heaven, we will want
to know where the Starbucks is.

You've blessed us to the point
we have high standards now.

So, we'll need high-speed wi-fi
and Whole Foods. And, let's see,
oh yeah, hypoallergenic pillows.

Just so you'll know.

Pandora's Book

> And I wept much, because no man
> was found worthy to open and to read
> the book, neither to look thereon.

~ Revelation 5:4

Which is why poetry sales
go ten to one to women—

and explains why we've got
a president who's never read
a book, including the one
ghost-written for him.

Besides, judging by
the hallucinogenic
quality of St. John's
writing in Revelation,

I'm not sure that the book
he's going on and on about
here, so early in Chapter 5,

would be all that great.

Lucky Number

> And I looked, and behold a pale horse:
> and his name that sat on him was Death,
> and Hell followed with him.
>
> ~ Revelation 6:8

Do I really have to say it?

Never in my life did I believe
that the Book of Revelation
had anything to do with
sanity, let alone reality,
or even prophecy.

But, behold…
that Fourth Rider
has arrived and is idly
fiddling with his pale tie
over a tepid cup of coffee
loaded with cream and sugar

on his "yuge" oak desk,
the biggest desk ever,
in the Oval Office.

Million-mile Stare

Saying, Hurt not the earth,
neither the sea, nor the trees,

~ Revelations 7:3

Ignoring the parts of the Bible
they don't care for, has to be
one of the longest-standing
traditions among Christians.

And it's fascinating the way
different scriptures go in
and out of style through
the eons and the ages.

Notice, now that we have
Walmart, Whataburger, and
Olive Garden, all sitting
on every other corner,

that Gluttony, as one
of Seven Deadly Sins,
is so out of fashion now.

What the priest doesn't know
about the Mediterranean Combo
or the Chop House Cheddar Burger
ain't gonna hurt either one of us.

But, when it comes to what
so many of the good little
bead-counters of the world

have done to the earth,
its seas, and the trees?

They're going to see
a million-mile stare
in the all-seeing eyes
on that Great White
Throne of Judgment,

right before they're cast
into the deep and wide
Lake of Eternal Fire.

A Moment of Silence

> And when he had opened the seventh
> seal, there was silence in heaven about
> the space of half an hour.
>
> ~ Revelation 8:1

This will be my favorite
30 minutes of the Apocalypse,
as long as that silence is extended
and offered to the earth as well.

For, even as far out as I am,
the noise of a gas chainsaw
echoes off the stone walls
of the granite mountains
on what would otherwise
be a rapturous morning.

There was no day in Genesis
on which God created the saw.

Only the trees did he make—
that we then used the curséd
tool of our own creation
to cut them all down.

So that 30 minutes
should be for us
to remember
the trees.

A Moment Later

After that silence though,
the seven angels will raise
the seven brass trumpets,
and the whole wide world
will go entirely to hell with

hail and fire mingled with blood
coming as soon as Verse 7.

Next, the trees and grass
go up in flames, and
a burning mountain
is hurled into the sea,
a sea that turns to blood,
while the fish begin to die.

Soon, a star called Wormwood
for some reason, falls to earth
and turns the waters bitter,

and the sun and the moon
start to fade, as the earth
grows darker than it was.

And this shit is too insane
for an apostle to conjure
without being altogether
stoned out of his mind.

Bite and Sting

> And they had hair as the hair of women,
> and their teeth were as the teeth of lions.

> ~ Revelation 9:8

I don't want to get into it
about ex-wives here...

but if Verse 10 goes on to say:

> And they had tails like unto scorpions,
> and there were stings in their tails:

what am I supposed to do?

Just not be honest and say,
that if the Book of Revelation
were still looking for leading ladies,
the mother of my daughter would be
an egregious act of typecasting?

And it wasn't only the teeth
and the sting in the tail—

it was the poisonous gas
in her emissions system,

along with the golden rod
of her fabulous disappointment,

not only in me, but an entire world

that never could measure up
to her divine standards.

And I am telling you that when
the second half of Verse 10 claims:

                              and their power was
                        to hurt men five months.

those men in the Apocalypse
are getting off easy.

So It Begins

> One woe is past; and, behold,
> there come two woes more hereafter.
>
> ~ Revelation 9:12

The woman from Pasadena
drags me out to her all-day
"Resistance Reading"...

You could take it from there.
But I think I'll go on anyway.

Because, if I am going to sit here
in the padded seats toward the back
for the overture of the Great Tribulation,
it seems like I should report the news.

And the girl-yelling-in-my-general-
direction, who kicked things off,
sounded like seven trumpets.

So, since one woe is now past,
I think we know what's coming.

Behold, Three Woes More

Then came the tweedy professor
who crawled out of his mouse hole
on the third floor of the English Dept.
to sing a drawn-out dirge in Vietnamese.

People clawing at the knots tightening
in their esophageal pipes. No relief.
Not even with the sad translation.

*   *   *

Then came the Native American
who mistook her indigenous roots
as being something of interest
…in and of themselves.

*   *   *

And then came the keynote
who took us so far beyond
the most capable attention
spans sitting among us,

    testing the limits
    of every syllable
    in the keyword
    ex-as-per-a-tion,

to the point that the audience
began to run out of emojis
to send all their friends
who were quite smart
to stay at home—

to the point that even
the woman from Pasadena
refused to speak about it
on the long drive back,

for having kept my mouth
shut the whole performance
and not giving her the chance
to react to what she knew
I wanted to say.

Trigger Words

> By these three was the third part
> of men killed, by the fire, and by
> the smoke, and by the brimstone,
> which issued out of their mouths.

> ~ Revelation 9:18

The laureate tells me
he was threatened
by a U.S. veteran
at a recent reading
he did in a bookstore.

I said, You were heckled,
I think you meant to say.

He said, Well, he mentioned
his pistol that was "handy"
in a nearby car or truck.

And I said, Okay then…
we'll go with threatened.

He went on to tell me—
as he is so prone to do—
that the guy went on to say,
when he got up for open mic,
that it was shameful to use poetry
as a weapon… and that the laureate
might ought to pick up a gun himself
and support our troops, instead of
running off at the hippie-mouth.

Now… I share nothing but
gratitude for our veterans—
except for two I have known
who were first-rate assholes.
But they're beside this point.

However, if you cannot see
the fundamentally wrong-
headedness of this man's
claim about the difference
between poetry and guns?
I suggest you just move on
to the next poem in the book.

Among the poets who are dead,
the ones we have read the longest
have, on many occasions, pissed off
popes and kings, or been beheaded,
exiled, imprisoned—and/or died
penniless in the streets of famous
cities that didn't give a shit about
the poet, or the loss to the world.

Do you think St. John the Divine
just hung out on the Isle of Patmos
because he liked the weather so much?

Dante pined for his hometown of Florence
for over twenty years. He was so exiled,
his sons weren't allowed to return.

The list is so long, I'm not even
going to offer a third example,
    which is standard protocol
    for the illustrative process.

I just want to say to the laureate,
You are, my son, headed for, sadly,
your own version of Purgatory because,
how many times do I have to tell you,
Stop going to damned open mics!

But to the crusty old crackpot
who threatened the laureate?
I would like to suggest this—

We thank you for your service.
However, your service does not
give you a free pass to continue
to dwell in a pit of ignorance.

And, since the laureate has
a close relative who served
as a United States Navy Seal,
to suggest he does not support
our troops is, simply put, moronic.

Otherwise, maybe spend more time
fingering the pages of great literature—
and less, fondling your semi-automatic dick.

Jesus Christ

The woman from Pasadena
is at therapy this afternoon
down in Santa Fe. She'll stay
the night with my daughter,

and there'll be a good deal
of post-therapeutic wine,
crying, and merry-making
at my expense, I am sure.

Even though the big issues
have to do with the bastard
in Pasadena who came before.

And I wonder how many sessions
it'll take, until she finally drops me
by virtue of being done with men.

And yet, how could I blame her
when she gets up the gumption.

Which has me thinking about
men and the biblical number
of our unpardonable offenses.

No wonder Jesus had to squat
and draw in the sand for a while
when those pharisaical assholes
brought him that adulteress.

I can hear him muttering
his own divine name
under his breath.

Met.a.phor

> And I took the little book out
> of the angel's hand, and ate it up;
> and it was in my mouth sweet as honey:
> and as soon as I had eaten it,
> my belly was bitter.
>
> ~ Revelation 10:10

Dangerous things happen
when people cannot grasp
that the Lord God might
have been a fan of drama,
imagery and metaphor—
a poet, for heaven's sake.

Somebody reads a few lines,
or a stanza back in the darker
corners of the Old Testament,

and suddenly, we've got a maniac
carving a tank-sized set of engraved
Ten Commandments out of marble
and ruining the well-cared-for grass
on the front lawn of the courthouse.

To add to it, we've got some junior
senator from the state of Georgia,
pushing legislation to make it legal,
who could not even remember—
when pressed by a reporter—
what six out of those ten
commandments are!

Next thing you know…
we've got denominations
that force children to fondle
deadly-poisonous reptiles.

Soon after comes the dude
who buys a 9-millimeter rifle
and starts shooting doctors
outside of women's clinics.

Folks—the Lord is a poet,
for God's sake. He likes
drama, symbol, imagery.

He uses met.a.phor.

Look it up.

Damnation

And he said unto me,
Thou must prophesy again
before many peoples, and nations,
and tongues, and kings.

~ Revelation 10:11

No prophet wants the hellish job.
If he does, he falsified his papers.

And I'm not saying that I'm one.
But, for me to do these books,
surely took the effort of one.

Thus it happens—a Trump
comes galumphing along...

and the reluctant curmudgeon
has to pull on his big-boy shorts

and address the damn peoples,
the damn nations, and damn
tongues, and the damn kings.

In This Manner

> and if any man will hurt them,
> he must in this manner be killed.
>
> ~ Revelation 11:5

I think of him often,
and the returns I would
commit upon him. Returns
that would do no good, not
for my daughter, not for me,
not for anything like justice.

These men stalk the earth.
If you kill one, another one
is born to a mother who had
some similar terrible thing
committed against her.

And I'd drop a mighty
God-sized fist to end this
repeating pattern if I could,
but if God hasn't stopped it,
I don't know how I would.

Still, when I come across
this biblical advice, I think
about the one who did it,

and the manner in which
I'd do it back to him.

We're Fired

Weather, Mother Nature's right hand,
is swinging a hard-cocked fist lately.

And though the verse above sounds
like just another day in the laureate's
home state, it's hard not to believe
that the earth and its atmosphere
are speaking straight to us now.

Lightning seems to be saying,
Enough! in every jagged flash
of its blazing electric sword.
Thunder grumbles after it,
And, prepare for great change!

Earthquakes are continents
shaking their aching shoulders
to rid themselves of us, like we're
a business of flies on a cow's flank.

And hail is just the future smacking us
on the shoulder, rapping on our skulls,
letting us know we screwed up, and so,
if we don't mind, or even if we do,
it will take over from here.

Pick Your Poison

To which I'd tend to say,
if it's just going to continue
up there, why not go to hell?

Down there, most likely,
everyone is drinking
and playing cards
and therefore,
getting along.

Van Gogh told us,
right before he died,
"The sadness will
last forever."

O Vincent…
if you only knew
how right you were.

That's why I'd take scotch
and one good game of poker
over the war of the righteous
any day of the week—or
for an eternity.

The Congregation

And the great dragon was cast out,
that old serpent, called the Devil, and Satan,
which deceiveth the whole world: he was cast out
into the earth, and his angels were cast out with him.

~ Revelation 12:9

It's important to remember
that demons were once angels—
angels cast down and out into the earth.

And they walk among us still, because
they were fruitful and did multiply.

And even with years of practice,
I continue to confuse the two.

I often forget—because of
their previous lives—one
might look like the other.

Because of his tailored suit,
and his finely-crafted ways
with words and witticisms,

we may not notice the nubs
of two horns parting the hair
on either side of his tight skull.

Because of her silken black hair,
mind-bending smile, and passion

for all the right books and plays,

we may not catch the occasional
flash of fire-red in the darkest
regions of her fabulous eyes.

And, in these dark days...

I fear the legions may be
slowly and imperceptibly
forming their ranks, and
going over their orders,

in preparation for
the final battle.

Whatever It Takes

> And to the woman were given two wings
> of a great eagle, that she might fly into
> the wilderness, into her place, where
> she is nourished for a time,
>
> ~ Revelation 12:14

Not quite to thirty yet,
and my daughter, I fear,
may have the tough work
still ahead.   And…
I don't know how to tell her.

A decent woman I went to see
for some professional help
    (because, yes, even old
    assholes seek advice)
asked me early on—

*What number of women
in the world do you think
have been sexually assaulted?*

I said that I didn't know,
but the number that lives
in my deepest suspicions
increases every other day.

She said, *Well then, take
your suspicious number
and double it, if not triple,
and you'll be on your way.*

My guess is that this kind
of talk is not standard
practice in her field.

She just knew that she
would have to work hard
and fast with the likes of me.
And, I respect her for that.

But, it did take me back
to the days of my youth
when prayer was a part
of my weekly routine—

and it made me want to ask
someone with more power
to please give my daughter
wings…
             that she might fly
into the wilderness—
into her place—

where she will be
nourished for a time.

The Great Denial

These are they which were not defiled
with women, for they are virgins.

~ Revelation 14:4

And we wonder where thousands of years
of priests molesting young altar boys
came from—that deeper sickness
of humankind? To be the ones
with dicks, and then to blame
the ones without for most
of our sad problems?

If Hillary Clinton,
during her campaign,
had been recorded saying
she could reach around and grab
any limp appendage she felt like
any time she felt like doing it,

we would have drowned her
in the nearest pond, and then
displayed her body from a tree
somewhere along the shoreline
in, say, Salem, Massachusetts.

But, The Don walks away
without a slap on the hand
that he uses to do the same.

Spare me your hollow offense
and gasp of holy indignation.

Growing up among the nuns
at Holy Angels, it took me
three to four decades just
to begin to believe that

the act of making love—
among the most beautiful
gifts granted by the God
they believe is there—

was not, actually...
an act of defilement.

And if I sound like
I am still bitter
about the betrayal,
                    I am.

Fallen

Babylon is fallen, is fallen, that great city.

~ Revelation 14:8

It was the parking garages
that did us in... well, that

and bridges... that and any
building over two stories tall.

Structural engineering students
in America stopped attending class
because they were bored... well, that

and fraternity parties... that and all
the batteries died in those special,
expensive calculators they used.

Turns out the best in every
department got kicked out
of the country because their
student visas expired... that,

and that they had come from
the wrong parts of the world.

Those parts that Trump put
on his special little black list.

We elected that homunculus,
because we were both dumb
and damn proud of it... well,

that... and, because poly-sci
majors are no longer required
to take basic courses in math.

And since we defunded the arts
and the humanities—and we cut
philosophy from the curriculum,

we could not see it coming.

Just Checkin' In

and they have no rest
day nor night,

~ Revelation 14:11

As a kid in the linoleum halls
of a church among graveyards,

I got the impression that helping
the poor was one of your big things.

But I have seen mostly good, and rare,
human beings doing the bulk of the work.

Soup kitchens and clothes closets... and,
Mother Teresa sure made a helluva dent.

But, as for you, personally, however,
considering all that power you have,

I thought I would just throw out,
in case you're not paying attention,

the poor are still very much with us,
and, in greatly increased numbers,

and, they have no rest
day nor night.

Losing Hope

And I saw another sign in heaven,
great and marvelous,

~ Revelation 15:1

and I've seen
what I thought
were a few of these,

but ultimately, they fell
a little flat, to be honest.

I thought a black man
becoming President
was a sign in heaven,
great and marvelous,

but all that came of him
was a white man ten times
worse than the white man
who had come before.

So, here we are,
hallelujah,
Amen.

Gnawing at Us

> and they gnawed their tongues for pain.
>
> ~ Revelation 16:10

As do we…
each time Trump,
or a press secretary,

strives to explain why
he just did what he did,
or just said what he said,

or, worse, tries to defend

> what
> the hell
> he just did.

From media executives
to a baffled press corps—

or in the halls of congress,
behind every slammed door
in the White West Wing—

the echoes of someone
screaming, "What!
in God's name
is he doing
now?"

Taijitu

I will tell thee the mystery of the woman,

~ Revelation 17:7

I appreciate the sentiment
behind the promise here,

but I don't feel any closer
to understanding her—

outside of the unavoidable
truth that if the Yang exists,

the Yin must be there also,
to complete the circle—

that dark and ever-cloudy
half of the endless swirl—

the half we can't see through,
even on the brightest of days.

And, half of me still desires
to understand the mystery.

But, the other half...
is letting go.

What *Will* We Do?

> And the fruits that thy soul lusted after are
> departed from thee, and all things which were
> dainty and goodly are departed from thee,
> and thou shalt find them no more at all.
>
> ~ Revelation 18:14

Imagine, like John Lennon,
the annihilation of "stuff."

No more QVC Home
Shopping Network.

No more mall kiosks
manned by bored teens
watching porn on phones.

No more cute clutch purses
or premium suede tote bags.

No shirts with stupidly clever
witticisms across the front—
or bright red Make America
Anything Again ball caps.

For, yes, it is coming—
what is written here—

behold the end of all
rhinestones and sequins,
sparkles, spangles, and glitter.

No more gold, silver, or bronze.
For, the earth hath been stripped
and mined of its precious metals.

Chain the doors of the big-box
stores. Convert the Walmarts
into churches, since prayer
is all that's left to us now.

Don your Sunday best,
for it shall surely be
your Sunday last.

All That Shines

For in one hour so great riches
is come to nought.

~ Revelation 18:17

May the God of our youth
find a way to save my sweet
sister from that golden asshole
she's married to in Los Angeles—

proof that riches can go to Purgatory
long before they ever come to nought.

One of my better friends growing up,
I miss her, and I wish she would
bail, like I was smart enough
to do, more than once.

But, great riches—
even in Purgatory—
have a wicked appeal,
cast a compelling spell.

Still, I must say, dear sis,
all great riches *will* come
to nought.   Eventually.

And I live here in the riches
of these mountains because
I believe that they will be
among the last to go.

Re-light

That's the saddest moment.
When the light goes out.

Like in me, the day
my daughter told me
about the day it went out
in her… several years back.

It's why we spend so much
time sitting by the fire pit
when she comes to visit.

We're looking for
the spark that
will do it.

Bon Vivant

You know who you are…

men-of-a-certain-suit dressed in
servant-of-the-people's clothing.

Pretending you are there for us,
when it's really for the kohlrabi
and aebleskivers they serve there
at Noma in Copenhagen, or maybe
the sturgeon under its cloche
at Eleven Madison Park
in New York City.

Don't try to kid us…

you're here for the new
private Learjet 45XR…

and the girls in bright red
silken dresses they provide
at no extra cost, of course,

in countries that continue
to have no problem at all
with the slow destruction
and desecration of human
life and the dignity of women.

You do your time for the camera
in a striped tie up on The Hill.

And each one of you leaves
in a separate stretch limo...

and each one of you knows—
down in the gold-lined pockets
you keep your manicured hands
fiddling around in while you fake
a smile at repulsively expensive
parties, galas, and soirees—

that every one of you bastards
is outnumbered more than
a million to one...

      and so...
    some day...

A Good Ride

Let us be glad and rejoice,

~ Revelation 19:7

because, what we've been
for these last 200,000 years
as humans has been so much
more interesting and, at times,
even fun, than had we remained
as apes among the bamboo stalks
and banana trees in the lowlands.

Nothing against the apes, mind you.
They never forgot some of the rules
and guiding principles that could have
given us another few thousand years.

But, they're not talking anymore...
not to us... since we have ravaged
and raped everything that matters
to them. And since we no longer
know how to speak the primary,
and truest, language of silence.

So, the binge party has finally
run out of beer and guacamole.

And it will end in fire, plagues,
a seven-headed dragon, and
insane weather patterns.

Yes, now come the laws
of reciprocity—the ways
of the universe and entropy.

And though humans had hoped
that maybe they'd be an exception,

our hubris, and narcissism,
will not be enough
to save us
now.

Slithering Around

And he laid hold on the dragon, that old serpent,
which is the Devil, and Satan,

~ Revelation 20:2

Symbol is symbol—
as metaphor is metaphor—
and for as long as phallic imagery
is, and has been, phallic imagery.

I'm with Justice Potter Stewart,
in a 1964 Supreme Court Order,
when he spoke of pornography:

"I know it when I see it."

And laying hold on the dragon
is about as phallic as anything
I have ever scanned, friends
and fellow English majors.

Of course, the Bible is rife
with fetishism and aberrant,
even bizarre, sexual behavior.
It's a big part of what gets a kid
interested in a religious practice.

But I'd not seen this verse before.
And now, it is my new favorite.

So I tried it out on the woman
from Pasadena the other day,

"Come dear, and lay hold on
the dragon, that old serpent."

She didn't speak to me the rest
of that day. Didn't touch me
again for a couple more—
as well she shouldn't have.

For, is not the ol' dragon
the low-down denominator
behind most of history's man-
made disasters and catastrophes?

    The Trojan War.
    Oedipus and Jocasta.
The Othello Syndrome.

Or, every other story
Shakespeare ever told.

And, let us not forget
the Garden of Eden—

that old serpent slithering
around in the undergrowth,
always showing up everywhere.

Sand of the Sea

> the number of whom is as
> the sand of the sea.
>
> ~ Revelation 20:8

the number of wasps
    and ants in Texas…

the number of televisions
    in bars and restaurants…

the number of poems in the world
    loved only by the poet
    who wrote them…

the number of people, plants, and animals
    that will be screwed over, or killed,
    by this president's policies…

the cups of coffee it took me
    to write these three books…

the number of miles I had to drive
    to know what to write in them…

the number of man-made noises
    that fill our dying atmosphere,
    like a cacophonous sonic smog…

the tears we'll cry when four billion of us
    run out of potable water…

the number of cockroaches
    and dung beetles that will
    thrive in the Apocalypse...

the flies and mosquitoes that won't
    give a damn when we are gone...

the number of cell phones that will rot
    among the ruins in the 135° heat...

the vast number of stars and planets
    that won't know of our passing...

the number of memories that
    cannot, ever, be erased...

the number of chances we had
    throughout human history
    to do better than we did...

and the number of minutes
    I've spent, so many wasted,
    contemplating all this crap...

Not Sure about That

> and there shall be no more death,
> neither sorrow, nor crying, neither
> shall there be any more pain:

> ~ Revelation 21:4

Sounds great, on the surface.

But through a magnifying glass,
there are some frightening little
critters crawling around on this
rather dramatic claim, it seems.

If we finger-thump the future,
according to this verse, we hear
a hollow and interminable ring.

Suddenly, we have no points
of reference for life, for joy,

for laughter, or the great way
that Valium or Vicodin feels
after the hemorrhoid surgery.

Sounds like a time when even
our best jokes could become
an absolute and endless hell.

No Exception

> And he said unto me, It is done.
>
> ~ Revelation 21:6

And I say unto him,
Famous last words, friend.

Because, if you haven't noticed,
from Greek tragedies to Proust,

and from priests to that one
asshole at every party—

endings tend to drag out.

I've learned to walk away
the moment I hear the words,

And wait, that's not even
the best part...

So, I have no reason
to believe that the end
of all things, and all time,
are going to be any different.

Omega Maybe

I am Alpha and Omega,
the beginning and end.

~ Revelation 21:6

Donald Trump was,
by no means, the Alpha—

though, he cannot imagine
anything of much interest
having come before him.

However, his chances
for being the Omega,

make him one of
the main players
we should keep
a keen eye on.

We All Fall Down

> according to the measure of a man,
>
> ~ Revelation 21:17

the fish has always been
well over two feet long
and weighed, at least,
thirty to forty or so
some odd pounds.

It's why dikes break
and skyscrapers collapse,
and bridges slowly crumble
into a waiting river below.

The measure of a man
has always been about
two to three inches off.

Ask any woman.

And this is why—
with Trump talking
about infrastructure—

we haven't a chance in hell.

Ad Nauseam

And I saw no temple therein:

~ Revelation 21:22

The only way
back to God now,
if he decides to wait,
would be to beat every
church into a ploughshare,

to turn every temple into
a memorial for all the sad
and burned-out angels who
had given heaven their best,

and, to make every mosque
a center for the advancement
and glorification of—as well
as the payment of restitution
to—women all over the world.

Otherwise, we will merely keep
attending, reciting, and praying.

And God will keep not listening.

Burn Baby Burn

> And the city had no need of the sun,
> neither of the moon, to shine in it:
>
> ~ Revelation 21:23

because they're burnin'
13,000 megawatts a day
in New York City, Baby,

expelling the black bones
of long-dead dinosaurs.

The city is a lamp
unto itself.

But...
someday...

the sun is going
to make them pay

for a hell of a lot more
than just the electric bill.

Gutless

and his servants shall serve him:

~ Revelation 22:3

To you, the spineless
tid-willies, the republican
senators and congressmen,
and, especially, women—who
continue to support the madness
of King Trump III, a man who
has not spoken a well-formed
sentence in all his adult life—
if the history books are kind
to you, it will be by virtue
of simply not bothering
to include your name.

And, the next verse
in the closing chapter
of this macabre book
of the Apocalypse says:

and his name shall be
in their foreheads.

So… remember this…
O red-tie-frump-bottoms
on the right side of the aisle:

Tattoos are damn painful
and costly to remove.

Tweet Tweet

> And I John saw these things,
> and heard them.
>
> ~ Revelation 22:8

Yes, John...

and "these things"
are why they throw us
into the Gulag in Siberia...
or kick us out of our countries.

And that is why they use us to test
new, experimental medications,

why our parents turn and bow
their heads, or our siblings
ask us not to come visit
their families anymore.

And, it is the reason
for the libel and slander
lawsuit of a former friend.

Or the president's late-night
tweets, sitting on the shitter.

It Gets Worse

And let's not forget
the filthy righteous—

those so holy we stride
a wide birth around them
at funerals and weddings—

because their mere presence
is a nagging reminder of all
the ways we've failed God.

As bad if not worse than
the righteously filthy—

the lying and insecure
demagogue-in-a-box,

who blithely believes
that, since demons
were once angels,

he must, by way of
his sick genealogy,
be an angel still.

Come Now

> And, behold, I come quickly;
>
> ~ Revelation 22:12

All the "That's what she said"
jokes aside, this is the reason
many of us have given up.

How many times must I say,
we're tired of hearing the end
is near. So... clap, clap!
Places everyone!

Fortyish years ago,
an idiot with a death
and resurrection wish
wrote a paperback book
by the title *88 Reasons Why
The Rapture Will Be In 1988.*

The laureate and I sometimes
enjoy laughing, through tears,
at some of the reasons he gave.

Anyway... I don't remember
a thing about 1988. My 30s
were a wash. And, the guy
who wrote the damn book,

finally died in 2001.

My Portion

and my reward is with me,

~ Revelation 22:12

The Bible promises many times
that we will get what we deserve.

A threat the nuns at Holy Angels
relished holding over my head.

And, as their vindictive joy
helped form the man I am,

I would say—setting aside
demeanor and disposition—

that, despite my inner ragings
over my daughter's tormenter,

and suffering a petty, insecure,
orange automaton as president,

that I have been an honest man.
Wave any of my words in God's

face on our Judgment Day, and I
will stand and take what he dishes.

The Great Excuse

And there you have it…
the root of all terrorism—

well, that, combined with mind-
numbing modern boredom
and violent video games—

that fear of whatever lies
outside of our best made
walls, plans, and bunkers.

It is religion's relentless
propaganda promoting
some one and only way.

The politician's perfect
and well-polished tool,
a ruthlessly-, relentlessly-,
clearly-defined "them."

The reason for all
our problems.

So It Goes

If any man shall add unto these things,
God shall add unto him the plagues
that are written in this book:

~ Revelation 22:18

Have I added anything
unto these sanctified words?

I've done nothing that priests
and theologians haven't done
over thousands of years.

They saw it their way.
I see it mine.

So it goes,

as Kurt Vonnegut says
too many times to count
in *Slaughterhouse-Five*.

The dim candle burns,
and we slave in its light
to fix what isn't broken.

So it goes.

We print the prophet's words
in books that few will read.

So it goes.

We believe in a certain version
of something over nothing.

We believe in it enough
to say we'll die for it.

    So it goes.

We claim a holy love
for our fellow man,
in the name of God,

with a pistol pointed
at the skull of some
other fellow man.

    So it goes.

        So it goes.

Give or Take Away

> And if any man shall take away from
> the words of the book of this prophecy,
> God shall take away his part
> out of the book of life,
>
> ~ Revelation 22:19

Have I taken away from
the words of this book?

I may have left a few
untouched, but that is
because they were just
too bizarre to deal with.

As I have hinted before,
good St. John the Divine
was probably partaking of
illegal substances long before
partaking of illegal substances
was made cool by the new laws
of Colorado and California—

and, before those substances
were made illegal, it seems
important to mention.

What would be unusual,
or wrong, about a prophet
smoking some weed on a rock
by the city gates, to try and calm
his nerves, what with all the crazy

and psychedelic revelations
God kept forcing on him.

But, here I've gone now
and added to the words
of this hallowed book.

So I'll be screwed
for addin' *and*
for takin'…
I suppose.

Sayonara... Au Revoir...

> The grace of our Lord Jesus Christ
> be with you all. Amen.
>
> ~ Revelation 22:21

Amen... Aloha... Namaste...
As-salamu Alaykum...
Shalom Aleichem...

Whichever is yours,
   go with it, Baby...
and may it be with you.

One misanthrope in the hand
is not worth two curmudgeons
in the bush. Just to be clear.

I wish very few people ill.
And, the very few I wish ill,
is for the betterment of others.

And I am not saying all politicians
and priests should be euthanized, but
maybe God could go Old Testament
again and break a few arms, maybe
throw some shit on their faces—
as he's said to do in Chapter 2
of The Book of Malachi.

The problem is, and
has always been,

that moderates are lazy,
and the liberals are stoned.

And crazy zealots are angry
because their God does not
permit them to drink wine.

As well they should be—
since their God is the one
who made it, from scratch,
and tends to drink it himself.

Therefore, why wouldn't they
turn out for the vote en masse?
They have nothing else to do.

The sad scene is pervasive,
and it's one that I cannot
do a damn thing about.

So, I go to the mountain.

Amen... Aloha... Namaste...
As-salamu Alaykum...
Shalom Aleichem...

Peace and solitude...
those are all I ask for—
and a good glass of scotch.

A misanthrope hates people,

a curmudgeon is just tired
of being around them.

There is a difference.

And so, I say:

May the grace
of God, Yahweh,
Allah, and Buddha

be with you all.

I don't have a short temper, I just have a quick reaction to bullshit.

~ Jimmy LaFave

Author Bio

Ezra Lipschitz was born in 1955, then mostly raised as a Catholic with a Jewish last name in Colma, California—a necropolis for the city of San Francisco.

He completed a degree in English at UC Davis—though, he does not recall getting his diploma—and now lives in a cabin at the foot of the Rocky Mountains in Southwestern Colorado near the border with New Mexico.

To earn what little money he requires, he travels around the Southwest playing folk songs in bars and coffee shops where he hopes to make enough money to buy a decent glass of scotch and some gas to get back home.

Apocalypse Soon: The Mostly Unedited Poems of Ezra E. Lipschitz is his third collection in a series. The first two are *I Shouldn't Say…* and *Arse Poetica*.

MEZCALITA
PRESS

An independent publishing company dedicated to printing and promoting the poetry, fiction, and non-fiction of musicians who want to add to the power and reach of their important voices.

www.ingramcontent.com/pod-product-compliance
Lightning Source LLC
Chambersburg PA
CBHW030005110426
42736CB00040BA/375